PREPARING F(
AMERICAN ASSAU]
AT SLAPTON SANDS, 1944

Revised Edition

Copyright ©
ORCHARD PUBLICATIONS

Originally compiled and published by Arthur L. Clamp titled *The American Assault Exercises at Slapton Sands, Devon, in 1944.*

ORCHARD PUBLICATIONS
2 Orchard Close, Chudleigh, Devon TQ13 0LR
Telephone: (01626) 852714

ISBN 1898964 67 X

Printed by
Hedgerow Print, Crediton, Devon EX17 1ES

Contents

Introduction

Sixty years and more have passed since American combat troops used Slapton Sands and the neighbouring countryside for full scale rehearsal exercises in preparation for the D-Day landings in Normandy, France, which eventually led to the collapse of Hitler's Germany and peace in Europe. This area of coast and land was selected as one of a series of training grounds which, in this case, was used because it closely resembled the landing beach, code named Utah Beach, situated on the Cherbourg peninsula. The American forces stationed in Devon and Cornwall were known as U Force, and were part of a much larger invading force which landed in France at five points on the 6th June, 1944.

This historic event and its subsequent success marked the closing stages of the Second World War. Never before had such a large and complex number of troops, drawn from different nationalities, assembled in this country for the purpose of launching a major cross-channel attack on an enemy and it is very unlikely that an event of this scale will ever be possible again as the means of detection by satellites would soon bring it to the attention of an opposing army.

Slapton Sands and its immediate land area played a very important part in this enterprise. Many people still recall the evacuation of all its inhabitants and livestock from many farms, villages and homesteads and the appearance of United States' troops engaged in realistic exercises in which many casualties occurred. This brief episode in the life of the South Hams has not been forgotten and enquiries from visiting Americans still show a continuing interest in this event.

In the preparation of this account of the exercises I was greatly helped by the American military archives in Washington, U.S.A., from which source came the photographs. My thanks go to them and to many others working in Devon and London libraries who gave advice and time willingly. Lastly this title is dedicated to those who lost their lives during the preparations for D-Day and to the local people whose homes and livelihood were disrupted during 1943 and 1944.

Arthur L. Clamp

For this revised edition Orchard Publications also acknowledge Robin Rose-Price and Jean Parnell for the use of additional photographs, previously reproduced in *The Land we left behind* and *400 years in Torcross - a Pictorial History*.

Preparations for D-Day Invasion

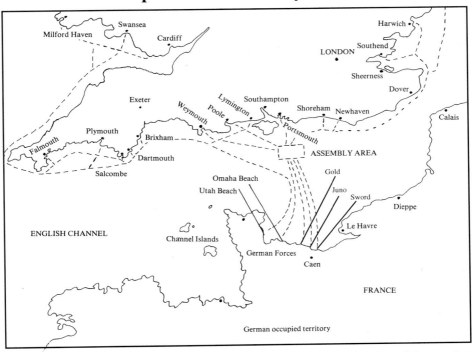

It was becoming evident to people in England during the middle years of the war that sooner or later an attack would take place somewhere on European soil to bring to an end Hitler's occupation of the Continent and his own downfall. Extensive fighting had been taking place on the Russian Front for two years and more and they were, quite naturally, pressing the Allies to open up a Second Front along the Western coast of Europe.

The idea of a cross-channel invasion of Europe had been considered as early as 1940 but it was not until January, 1943, that, at a conference of Heads of Allied Governments in Casablanca, a firm decision was taken to launch a Second Front in the spring of 1944. Hitler's forces in North Africa were on the retreat by this time, a considerable build up of troops and military equipment was taking place in England, the Americans were shipping vast supplies from the States and troops were becoming available for other duties away from the Mediterranean theatre of war.

This enormous build up of men and supplies was an exceptionally well planned operation the purpose of which was only fully known to a few senior military and Government personnel. Co-ordination between hundreds of units, thousands of troops, both land and air based, soon resulted in England almost becoming a vast arsenal of supply dumps which were very carefully camouflaged and scattered throughout the land. Troops of many nationalities were involved and support was being planned by the French resistance movement behind the German lines.

5

This final assemblage of forces for the planned invasion was immense. Nothing had ever occurred on this scale in England; the whole country was poised for an attack on what was known as the Fortress of Europe.

General Eisenhower smiling at the invasion's success

There were in readiness 1,213 warships, including seven battleships and twenty three cruisers, 4,126 landing craft, 1,600 ancillary and merchant ships, 11,500 aircraft and 3,500 gliders. The allied army numbered 3½ million men of whom 1½ million were Americans. Nearly 150,000 troops were to be put ashore on D-Day alone. Almost the full length of the southern coast was declared a military zone through which movement of civilians was restricted and information about any aspect of military matters kept secret.

During the early months of 1944 plans were well in hand for the overall structure of the invasion plan and the preparation of land and air based troop movements leading to various departure points facing the English Channel. Operation Overlord was to be undertaken by five assault forces, two comprising of American troops and three of British and other troops. Five designated areas between Cherbourg and Le Havre along the coast of Normandy were code named and allocated one to each force. Airborne troops would be the first to land in France paving the way for the full scale landings in the early hours of 6th June, 1944, a date that had yet to be finally arranged.

The American forces were mainly situated in the West Country and divided in two assault groups 'U' and 'O' (to land at Utah and Omaha Beaches) followed by force 'B' which was mainly in camp around Falmouth and Plymouth. Assault force 'U' was concentrated around Salcombe, Dartmouth and Brixham in South Devon and assault force 'O' was in the Portland, Weymouth and Poole areas of Dorset. The United States. 1st Division was responsible for the Omaha landing and the United States 4th Division for the Utah landing. The United States Airborne Divisions 82nd and 101st were to be dropped inland from these beaches during the cover of darkness preceding the first light landings.

The British, Canadian and other troops were divided into assault forces 'G', 'J' and 'S' which were to land on beaches, code named Gold, Juno and Sword some miles east of the American landings. They were mainly stationed in the Hampshire area at Southampton, Portsmouth, Shoreham and Newhaven.

Both American and British airborne troops, aircraft and gliders were working towards a state of readiness on permanent and temporary airfields throughout southern England.

6

These would be the first troops to land in occupied France and their task was to capture certain key positions close to the beach landings and then to link up with ground troops after beacheads had been established and a way made clear for the follow up forces to move inland. The command structure of this giant operation came under General Eisenhower who was the Supreme Allied Commander assisted by Air Chief Marshal Sir Arthur Teddar as his deputy. The American Western Naval Task Force came under Rear-

American infantry on one of their last exercises in southern England a few weeks before D-Day.

Admiral A. G. Kirk, U.S.N., aboard U.S.S. Augusta while Rear-Admiral D. P. Moon, U.S.N., was responsible for assault force 'U' and Rear-Admiral J. L. Hall, Jr., U.S.N., for assault force 'O'. General Sir Bernard Montgomery, back from the successful North African campaign, took charge of the overall landings and breakthrough inland.

The stage for launching the cross-channel invasion was nearly ready. The original plans had been modified by Montgomery and the final ones were accepted on 15th May, 1944, at his headquarters in Hammersmith. The audience, which included Winston Churchill and King George VI, heard that the landings were to be made by two divisions of the United States First Army under the command of Lieu;-General Omar N. Bradley and three divisions of the British 2nd Army led by Lieut-General Sir Miles Dempsey.

As the days and weeks passed during the spring of 1944 troops and supplies were being assembled in concentration areas, equipment not required for the immediate landings was left behind and by the 26th May the actual assault troops were camped in marshalling areas. These were sealed in camps where briefings took place although the exact place and time of the invasion was still withheld. Up to this date only senior staff were aware of the precise nature of the attack and this was only made known to the troops when they were crossing the Channel. Some 170 million maps, diagrams and plans were issued during the last hours before the French coast was reached.

Special points of embarkation had been set aside and 'hards' were constructed over which heavy vehicles and equipment could be taken into landing ships and craft. One hundred and thirty of these had been laid over beaches which enabled tanks and lorries etc, to cross safely. In order to keep the equipment and supplies dry during the crossing, every major item had to be waterproofed, and then de-waterproofed after landing. The actual day and time for the invasion had still to be finalised as weather conditions would play an important part in the success of this operation.

Unsettled weather conditions did cause some delay at the last moment. It had been decided to time the invasion for first light on the 5th June, 1944, but a last minute forecast caused a change of date. However, with some troops already set to sea and a break in the weather was anticipated Operation Overlord was set on course for landing at 06.30 hours on Tuesday, 6th June, 1944.

Allied Invasion Chiefs in conference. Left to right: General Bradley, Admiral Ramsey, Air Chief Marshal Tedder, General Eisenhower, General Montgomery, Air Chief Marshal Leigh-Mallory, and General Smith.

Landing Crafts

The very large operation required a number of specialised craft for carrying troops and equipment across the Channel. Landing craft infantry (large) was designed for holding 200 men and had a speed of fifteen knots. Landing craft tank was a specially adapted craft designed to carry heavy tanks or vehicles right up to a beach. Landing craft assault was an armoured craft of ten tons capable of holding thirty six men and their equipment and landing them over a ramp in its bow. Landing craft vehicle and Landing craft personnel are, as their names indicate, craft adapted for particular uses taking loads right up to the beaches.

The Evacuation of the South Hams

G.I.s help with the packing of a very delicate rood screen in one of the churches. Many of these screens were riddled with wood worm and were extremely fragile.

As part of the necessary preparation for the successful invasion of German occupied France, it was vitally important that all troops had to undergo a series of training schedules and then full-scale exercises under conditions as near resembling those of the five landing points in Normandy as possible.

Slapton Sands and the immediate landward area was one of four major exercise areas designated for specialised use with live ammunition. Hayling Island, Bracklesham Bay and Littlehampton were the three other main training areas which came under strict military rule from the end of 1943 to the autumn of 1944. Slapton Sands with its small ley, low cliffs at either end of the flat coast road was not all that dissimilar from the beach and cliffs code named Utah west of the River Vire in Normandy. It was smaller, had fewer fortifications but was well away from German planes crossing the Channel towards the more populated areas of England.

A notice of requisition was passed to the Devon County Council under the Defence Regulations Act of 1939 specifying that a certain area of the South Hams was to be fully evacuated of civilians and livestock by the 20th December, 1943. This gave six weeks notice for the moving of about 750 families, comprising about 3,000 people, 180 farms, villages, shops, etc. Some 30,000 acres would have to be cleared in these weeks so that troops could move in and start setting up camps, defence points and ringing the area with guards.

The area took in the villages of Torcross, Stokenham, Chillington, Sherford, East Allington, Blackawton, Strete and Slapton and many hamlets. The requisitioned land covered the coast from just north of Strete to just south of Torcross and formed a diamond like area. All movable possessions from homes, shops and farms were to be taken and useable crops still in the land could be removed. Nothing was to be left apart from empty buildings and churches.

Meetings were convened in the various village halls telling people of the plans and how they could get help in the form of packing cases, transport and food and assistance with the actual work of handling heavy furniture, farm equipment and livestock. The people were naturally taken back by the order to evacuate but it was wartime and almost anything could take place. Plymouth had suffered a devastating blitz, young children were living in the area as evacuees, husbands were at war so this move, it was explained, however difficult, upsetting and inconvenient it would be was necessary and would make a very practical contribution to training troops to win the war.

Two information centres were set up at Blackawton and Stokenham and staffed by the Women's Voluntary Service. Help was forthcoming from many people throughout Devon and offers of accommodation given while farmers roundabout shared fields and equipment with those who lost their land. Advice was given about obtaining help, seeking alternative accommodation and storing furniture and goods. Emergency kitchens were able to supply meals to those in the middle of moving; transport, in one way or another, was made available for moving out tons of domestic and farming goods to many parts of the West Country.

There were, of course, difficulties especially with the elderly folk many of whom had never left the area before and with sick people where it was necessary to find them beds in nearby hospitals. These and many other problems were overcome by a willingness on most people's part to pull together and make the most of it. The war was on and this was one consequence of the times.

As the few weeks passed so the land and villages took on a deserted appearance. The once crowded roads down to the shore, the busy farms, the cattle grazing the fields, the people talking in the village shops were to be no more. The large villages were soon empty then came the many farms and finally the isolated houses. The various churches had to be cleared of valuables and very old furnishings. No guarantee that anything left would be undamaged during the exercises. Treasures such as crucifixes, silver crosses and plateware were carefully packed by experts and monuments, windows and fittings were protected by sandbags. Almost all the churches had a lot of old and fragile woodwork. This required very careful dismantling and packing helped in many cases by the incoming U.S. troops. The inns closed their doors for the last time and the cellars were emptied of their stocks of cyder and beer.

During the last few days of the evacuation sentries came into the area, American officials checked on the clearing operation, the last people left taking with them as much of their crops as possible and finally the centres closed and the volunteers moved out. A silence fell over the area, an uncanny feeling that this was the lull before the storm. Weeds soon appeared in unattended gardens and fields, hedgerows grew out of shape and houses, farms and other buildings quickly gathered dust during those last days of 1943.

Alan and Bernard Fardon, whose father was the blacksmith in Blackawton, help out with a wheelbarrow.

Russell Lucas is collecting the last few items from a house in the narrows at Chillington. All the houses were locked up as the owners left and they were told that no one would go into them. However many of them were used and left in poor condition.

The Americans move in and the locals move out.

U.S. Troop Exercises at Slapton Sands

Exercise Fox: l0th to l2th March. Bombardment by two cruisers and eight destroyers.

Exercise Muskrat: 24th to 27th March. Bombardment by two cruisers and U.S.S. Bayfield (Rear Admiral Moon).

Exercise Beaver: 29th to 31st March. Bombardment by two cruisers and four destroyers.

Exercise Trousers: l lth to l3th April. Details not known.

Exercise Tiger: 26th to 29th April. Bombardment by two cruisers and seven destroyers.

Exercise Fabius: 3rd to 6th May. Bombardment by U.S.S. Augusta, H.M.S. Glasgow and nine U.S. destroyers.

Some of the exercises were witnessed by high ranking ofiicers including General Eisenhower and General Montgomery and V.I.P.s including Winston Churchill.

During the opening weeks of 1944 Slapton Sands and area became the scene of great activity with troops coming in setting up posts, defence positions, converting some buildings to observation points and preparing obstacles along the beach and main road. The whole area soon took on the appearance of a large military range with guns in position, signal stations working, encampments for the troops and vehicles and supplies stored in depots.

The area had been sealed off completely to civilians and only those with special permits were allowed in or could work close by such as coastguards and local homeguards who were responsible for maintaining watch along the nearby cliffs.

It soon became apparent to people living close by that something special was going to happen here as the large number of troops and their supplies could not be completely kept out of sight when approaching the area. People were asked not to say anything to anyone about what they saw or heard and troops when allowed out of the area while off duty were likewise warned of casual talk.

There were also American troops with equipment and supplies stationed at nearby Salcombe, Dartmouth and Brixham but these local areas were not barred to civilians in the same way as the Slapton Sands area. There was plenty of movement between these local stations and many lanes and some roads had to be widened or straightened to cope with the large amount of transport and the size of many military vehicles. It became very clear after a month or two that Slapton would play a very special role in the preparation of forces for the invasion of Europe although at this point in time nobody knew of the exact intentions of all this military activity or when it would leave South Devon on its mission to clear Europe of Hitler's troops.

Top secret communication.

Troops of assault forces 'U' and 'O' stationed throughout the West Country were, during the early months of 1944, engaged in a series of very specialised training schemes at selected areas in Devon and Cornwall and along the coast towards Weymouth. These minor exercises were to test various pieces of equipment, procedures and the demolition of obstacles prior to staging a small landing or attacking a given target. One centre was at Braunton in North Devon, the United States Assault Training Centre, where infantry battalions undertook training in amphibious techniques, the reduction of 'hedgehog' defences on beaches and attack tactics on fortified gun emplacements. These exercises were designed to test the efficiency of equipment and the effectiveness of small battalions of troops from which experience was gained and some modifications made to equipment and methods of attack.

Meanwhile other troops were undergoing a series of hardening exercises on Dartmoor, a terrain which is difficult to cross especially under poor weather conditions when much of it can soon be covered in cloud. Every effort was made during these preliminary exercises to make them as realistic as possible through the use of live ammunition over the heads and immediately in front of troops.

At the completion of these localised movements Divisional Commanders were briefed on the next stage of training when the whole of assault forces 'U' and 'O' would engage in two separate full scale rehearsals at Slapton. Towards the end of April, 1944, Operation Tiger took place with force 'U' and at the beginning of May Operation Fabius followed with force 'O'. Both exercises were conducted under conditions simulating as closely as possible those expected in the actual D-Day landings. The troops were not informed of the real purpose of these although no doubt many guessed their true nature and some, it was reported, actually thought that when they had embarked and set course towards the South Devon coast they were on the way to France. The rehearsals were organised and conducted with all the detail and thoroughness of the actual invasion. Landing craft were assigned from various bases along the South Devon coast to carry troops and equipment on a sea journey of the same length and time as it would take to cross the Channel to France. Assault teams were made up and plans of the rehearsal, objectives to reach and the conditions under which the troops would be landing were made known.

Within the very tight restrictions imposed by security along the whole of the English coast both exercises were to embody every detail that would be required for the landings on the Normandy coast. Troops were assembled in marshalling areas, briefed on their mission, taken to loading hards and assigned to the appropriate landing craft. The number of men involved and the manner of their grouping and use of equipment was exactly as it would be for the real operation. A course was set along the south coast to approximate the length of the channel crossing and the timing of departure and subsequent landing on the pebble beach at Slapton was to follow the prepared schedule for D-Day. The sea journey

Landing craft all loaded and ready to go. Was this the real thing or another practice run?

was to be covered by air support and under the control of the U.S. Navy.

Disembarkation was also to be covered with air and naval support preceded by preparatory bombardment of the coastal area while the troops were being taken towards the shore in the early hours of their assigned landing day. Naval vessels would be stationed in Start Bay to soften up positions along Slapton beach minutes before the troops were to land.

So the scene was set in this part of normally quiet Devon when people would often look out to sea and watch a few fishing boats go by or an occasional large boat on the horizon. Many of them must have been very surprised to see numerous landing craft coming into the area during the last days of April and the first few of May during that eventful year of 1944. If the craft could not be seen from away from the coast the attack by ships and planes could certainly be heard for many miles over the Devon countryside. It would be soon obvious to the local people that a large scale military exercise was under way and that this was a foretaste of a later event to take place somewhere in Europe.

A variety of objectives had been set up along the beach and its immediate landward area. These included gun emplacements, defended buildings, a dummy aerodrome and other features to resemble those to be expected on the Normandy coast. The beach assault forces were to use live ammunition and, of course, come under live fire from attacking planes and ships while moving towards the shore. Smoke screens were to be used as well to cover troop movements up the beach and ground units were to call in support from fighter and medium bombers to destroy obstacles in their way.

Operation Tiger was planned from 26th to the 29th April and involved troops stationed between Torbay and Plymouth, that is assault force 'U'. Major troop units involved were the 4th Infantry Division and the 82nd and 101st Airborne Divisions with support from other units. D-Day was planned for 27th April and the attack on the coast for first light of that day. The first object was to secure a beach-head and then make a rapid advance inland to secure certain objectives. The exercise finished on 29th April and the troops then returned to their various marshalling areas.

This first rehearsal was very successful and from it a number of co-ordinating lessons were learnt and then applied to the real invasion. One incident, however, marred this event. Two German E-boat flotillas totalling nine boats managed to pass the defending ships (there had been some last minute changes causing a weakness in the security) and stumbled on the exercise taking place during the hours of darkness. Two landing craft full of troops were sunk and one was damaged causing the death of about 700 men - more than were killed on Utah beach itself during the actual invasion. Such is the irony of war! The loss of the craft was critical to the Overlord assault lift as these craft were already in short supply. The Germans realised that they had sunk landing craft but fortunately did not conclude that they were part of a large military exercise.

Operation Fabius was planned along similar lines to Tiger and took place during the early days of May, 1944. The participating troops came from the Dorset area and comprised of units designated assault force 'O'. The objectives of the rehearsal were the same and the conditions under which it took place were to be as realistic as possible. The sea journey was also to be of the same length as that of the Channel crossing with troops and ships being accompanied by planes and ships.

Once again the Slapton Sands area came under attack procedure on fortified beach defences. This was immediately followed by waves of troops being brought into the area by landing craft and then staging an assault on the beach and penetrating inland as fast as possible towards given objectives.

So the days of Slapton Sands usefulness as a training ground came to an end when the smoke had cleared and the noise and activity had finally ceased. All was now ready for the real invasion of Europe to take place within a month of the ending of the two exercises.

Operations room.

Top secret communication re Exercise Tiger.
Supreme Headquarters Allied Expeditionary Force G-3 Division

SHAEF/23036/8/Trg   19 April 1944.

Subject: Exercise Tiger.

To:

1. Exercise TIGER will involve the concentration, marshalling and embarkation of troops in the TOR BAY - PLYMOUTH area, and a short movement by sea under the control of the U.S. Navy, disembarkation with Naval and Air support at SLAPTON SANDS, a beach assault using service ammunition, the securing of a beachhead and a rapid advance inland.

2. Major troop units are the VII Corps Troops, 4th Infantry Division, the 101st and 82nd Airborne Divisions, 1st Engineer Special Brigade, Force "U" and supporting Air Force units.

3. During the period H-60 to H-45 minutes, fighter-bombers attack inland targets on call from the 101st AB Div and medium bombers attack three targets along the beach. Additional targets will be bombed by both fighter-bombers and medium bombers on call from ground units. Simulated missions will also be flown with the target areas marked by smoke pots.

4. Naval vessels fire upon beach obstacles from H-50 to H-hour. Smoke may be used during the latter part of the naval bombardment both from Naval craft by 4.2" chemical mortars and at H-hour by planes, if weather conditions are favourable. Naval fire ceases at H-hour.

5. The schedule of the exercise is as follows:

	22 April	Move to marshalling area commences.
D-Day	27 April	101st AB Div simulates landing. Preparatory bombardment by air and navy. Assault landing and advance of 4th Div.
	28-29 April	Advance of 4th Div & 101st AB Div continues. 82nd AB Div simulates landing, secure and holds objective.

(Exercise terminates on 29 April)

6. Joining instructions will be issued later.

                                        W. R. PIERCE,
                                        Colonel, G.S.C.,
         TOP SECRET   Chief, Training, Sub-Section.
This paper must not be taken out of this
Headquarters except as laid down in Para. 27,
SHAEF Inter-Division Standing Security
Regulations dated 9 February 1944.

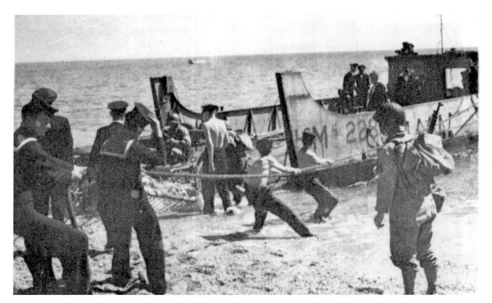

Craft coming ashore on Slapton Beach.

Shell crater in front of the remains of the Royal Sands Hotel, Slapton.

Troops march past the remains of the Royal Sands Hotel, which had been used for target practice.

These pictures and pages nos 23, 24, 25 and 26 show various aspects of the exercises in Start Bay. Landing craft can be seen coming in under a smoke screen, assembling off shore, then landing on the beach. A tractor is hauling craft up the steep pebble beach and soldiers can be seen cutting their way through the wire defences to form a beachead.

Troops and craft coming ashore at the far end of Slapton Beach.

Landing craft coming in and troops securing the beachead (below).

Once the beachead was secured heavier equipment came ashore.

A pontoon bridge was built across Slapton Ley.

Troops cutting their way through the wire defences.

U. S. Landings in Normandy, France, 6th June, 1944

The first troops from England to embark on this historic mission were the large American assault forces stationed along the coast of the West Country. Force 'U' from Salcombe, Dartmouth and Brixham, Force 'O' from Portland, Weymouth and Poole and the follow up Force' B' from Plymouth and Falmouth were given orders to get under way on the 30th and 31st May and 1st June. All troops and equipment were on board by the 3rd June from which date the exact positions of attack were given although the precise day had still not been finalised due to very unsettled weather conditions.

Force 'U' was divided into twelve convoys which made their way along the coast towards Weymouth where Force 'O' was putting to sea in five convoys (see page 5). Both assault forces followed a parallel route making for what was called the 'spout' an area of sea to be cleared of enemy mines through which all the five assault forces would have to pass before reaching the French coast.

All the Chiefs of Staff were at headquarters in Portsmouth where up to the minute weather forecasts were coming in. During Sunday morning, 4th June, 1944, General Eisenhower decided to postpone the invasion for twenty-four hours although the two convoys were on course across the Channel. They were ordered to return to Weymouth Bay and await further instructions. On Sunday evening another weather report indicated an improvement in conditions upon which advice General Eisenhower gave the final order to launch the invasion in the early hours of Monday morning - Operation Overlord was under way!

American troops heading across the Channel.

D. Day. Landing on the Normandy beaches.

The seventeen American convoys put to sea again and the British assault forces also got under way from various other points further up the Channel. American destroyers left their berths at Belfast, Ireland, on course for the battle zone and Airborne troops were boarding planes in many parts of England in readiness for their dropping points in Normandy now scheduled for the very early hours of Tuesday morning, 6th June, 1944.

While the U.S. Airborne troops were being dropped in the Cotentin area and British paratroopers near Caen, the invasion fleet was bringing the main body of the Allied armies to the Normandy shores. Mine sweepers cleared and marked ten lanes through enemy mines, fighter squadrons were above the convoys, there was still a low cloud level and the sea still very choppy. The crossing was uneventful and the Germans appeared to be unaware that anything unusual was taking place.

Approximately 13,000 bombs were dropped by 329 B-24 bombers on and around Omaha Beach and 293 planes softened up the defences on Utah Beach in a similar and more successful fashion as visibility was better in this area. At about 02.30 hours the headquarters ships were on station in the battle zone and troops were unloading into LCVP's that would take them to the beaches. At 05.45 the naval bombardment commenced from the destroyers and finished only minutes before the first troops from Force 'U' landed on Utah beach at 06.30. It was only a matter of minutes before the bombardment ceased that the defending Germans spotted the approaching forces.

It was too late to bring any major units up to defend the coast. The coastal batteries had already taken a hammering and now they were under close fire by the first waves of infantry coming ashore followed by engineer and demolition parties. The Utah beach landings were well established after just three hours of fighting and tanks, vehicles and

Utah Beach was taken with little opposition but om Omaha Beach the troops met with fierce resistance. Over 3,000 men died on this beach, the worst casualties of the whole operation.

numerous support equipment was being quickly brought ashore from which point breakouts were taking place with relative ease. There were few casualties at this point and the plans were more or less put into operation as laid down. 23,250 men went ashore on the first day with 1,742 vehicles and 1,695 tons of stores.

However, the picture on the Omaha Beach was quite different. The bombing had been largely off target due to poor visibility, the infantry transports were swamped by high waves, a lot of equipment was lost and the first troops ashore were there mainly without support from howitzers and other guns. The German defences were still intact and consequently were able to pin down the infantry on the beach for much longer than was planned. Out of the five landings in the invasion this one was most difficult. Additional supplies had to be brought in and it was only after four or six hours of the most gruesome fighting that German bunkers were slowly put out of action and a beachead was established. Some 3,000 died on this beach, the worst casualties of the whole operation.

Allied troops coming ashore.

These defences , known as hedgehogs, often had mines attached to them and were a deadly peril when submerged.

Over the next few days following the initial assault thousands more troops and equipment came ashore.

The South Hams Today

Many years have passed since the last American troops left this part of South Devon for the Normandy beaches in June, 1944. It was not until well into the autumn of the same year that people started returning to their farms and houses, some finding their properties intact while others were grieved to find considerable damage both to buildings, walls, hedges and even outbuildings. In spite of much hardship compensation for damage was given and assistance offered towards moving and settling in again. The information centres were reopened and after the area had been cleared of mines and military debris many families were back in their former homes by the end of the year and a start had been made on farming the land.

Some buildings which had been completely destroyed were not rebuilt including the Royal Sands Hotel which stood close to the beach by the road going up to Slapton village. A few of the churches had also been quite badly damaged and teams of experts were soon working on their restoration. Likewise the villages suffered, especially Strete although Torcross, in spite of its closeness to the sea, was relatively unharmed. Slapton Ley had been neglected, waterways choked with weeds and hardly any wildlife left except for rabbits which were found to be in great numbers over the whole area.

A granite obelisk now stands on the beach midway between Torcross and Strete which commemorates this episode in the life of the South Hams and the sacrifices made by the local people. It was unveiled on the 24th July, 1954, and presented by the United States of America. In spite of all the damage to buildings, trees, hedges and roads, hardly any scars remain from this period. There are occasional reports of shells being found and divers have located vehicles and other military equipment in the sea close to the shore.

24th June, 1954. The dedication of the monument which was presented by the U.S. Army in gratitude to the people of the South Hams.

Many visitors come to this area each year or pass through on their way to Kingsbridge or Salcombe. Some stop to read the lettering on the obelisk and ask questions about those far off days during the war. Many American visitors are curious about the area and some are pleased to find reminders such as the Normandy Inn, Blackawton, which contains photographs and some military relics.

The local people have not forgotten their part in the last war and the sacrifices they made in enabling this land to be used as a training battlefield in preparation for the Normandy invasion.

During the early 1970s Ken Small, a local guest house owner and avid beachcomber along Slapton Sands, heard of an 'object' lying on the sea bed about three quarters of a mile out to sea in sixty feet of water. A subsequent dive confirmed the 'object ' was an American Sherman tank, which was obviously lost during Exercise Tiger.

From that moment Ken Small was obsessed with the idea of raising the tank from the sea bed and bringing it ashore. His efforts are recalled in the book he wrote in 1988 titled *The Forgotten Dead*. The bureaucracy and red tape he encountered and overcame during the next ten years was enormous and many an individual would have given up several times over. Ken's obsession was to have the tank raised before the fortieth anniversary of D.Day and his efforts were rewarded when he finally managed, with much help, to have it winched ashore. Ken described it as a miracle but as the tank tracks hit solid ground away from the beach shingle they immediately engaged and started to turn. The tank was towed to a parking area in Torcross and today stands proudly in memory of all those soldiers and sailors who lost their lives on that terrible night - 28th April 1944.

The Sherman tank comes ashore after being submerged for nearly forty years.

34

The tank now stands alongside the car park, Torcross, as a permanent reminder of all the soldiers and sailors lost during Exercise Tiger.